TRI-ANEW-ANGLE

BERMUDA

ROY-ALLAN BURCH

Tri-Anew-Angle
Bermuda

iUniverse books may be ordered through booksellers or by contacting:

iUniverse
1663 Liberty Drive
Bloomington, IN 47403
www.iuniverse.com
1-800-Authors (1-800-288-4677)

Because of the dynamic nature of the Internet, any web addresses or links contained in this book may have changed since publication and may no longer be valid. The views expressed in this work are solely those of the author and do not necessarily reflect the views of the publisher, and the publisher hereby disclaims any responsibility for them.

Any people depicted in stock imagery provided by Getty Images are models, and such images are being used for illustrative purposes only. Certain stock imagery © Getty Images.

ISBN: 978-1-5320-7621-3 (sc)
ISBN: 978-1-5320-7622-0 (e)

Library of Congress Control Number: 2019906897

Print information available on the last page.

iUniverse rev. date: 06/04/2019

The wound is the place where light enters you - Rumi

Dedications

To the memory of
Russell Allan James Lister (May 19, 1933 - January 27, 2001)
Karen Francis Marie Burch (February 9, 1958 - October 22, 2003)
Frances H. Eve Lister (August 3, 1934 - May 13, 2019)

To Lauren, Serena, Xavier, Allison E., Conrad, Raishun and to family, friends, and coaches
who have supported me along the way.

To Bermuda and her people.

Special mention to Raph and Laney

The Broken Olympian

Introduction

This book is a culmination of insights learned during my Olympic journey. Over twenty-two years I trained, traveled, and competed for the Bermuda National Swim Team.

When I was eight years old (1993), my mother was diagnosed with stage four breast cancer. Her diagnosis sent me deep into the swimming world. Unbeknownst to me at the time, it was an outlet for frustration, confusion, and anger. In the water I could think about her and forget anything my body was feeling. When we are innocent we understand turmoil without the full context. I had little understanding of the journey she would endure but would come to understand her pain later on in life.

Through my early teen years, my strength in the water was recognized by local coaches. A path was created to enhance my growth as a student-athlete, although this was somewhat fallacious, as I was more of an athlete-student. I was willingly sent away to boarding school in September of 2002 to create bigger opportunities.

In October 2003 (senior year), I received a call from my mother explaining her treatment was no longer successful. This would be one of the most devastating moments of my life. Within days, I flew back to Bermuda. Upon seeing her, it was clear that this was the end for her. Listening to her struggle still resonates with me. I sat by her side for the better part of a week and my time had come to an end. Her stoicism prevailed as she sent me back to school. Reluctantly, I left her side filled with my own emotions of pain, sadness, anger, and despair. Three days later, just before midnight, I received a call from my grandmother explaining that my mother had passed on. Immediately, I erupted into tears, dropping the phone due to the numbness that overcame my body.

Arrangements were made for me to travel home and attend my mother's funeral. I spent a foggy week on the island before returning to school. For the next month I worked my way back into a routine but my core being was destroyed. I didn't seek any grief management or even have the understanding that it was necessary. Training became robotic and forced along with most of my life. When attending classes, my mind was elsewhere and my grades plummeted. Everything school orientated was about survival. My mental health was deteriorating while I internalized everything, so it may not have been apparent that anything was wrong.

I failed to secure a spot at University despite finishing the swim season as a top recruit. There was a technical mistake as a graduate from my former school, not allowing me to use grades accumulated at Peddie. My swimming abilities couldn't outshine my appalling academics. I later learned about the NCAA clearinghouse but it was too late. The two years spent at the institute became a wash.

My aim to compete at the 2004 Athens Olympics was dismantled by my inability to train. Barely attending practice, I took a hiatus from the sport after graduation. The summer following my senior year would be a far cry from the path initially set upon. For over two months, alcohol would become a crutch from dusk till dawn. Mixed with irregular sleeping hours, I lost nearly fifteen pounds. My body was rapidly wasting away from increased substance abuse and poor eating habits.

In mid-July 2004, by some miracle, I received a call from John Taffe, the head coach at Springfield College. He worked some magic and secured me a spot at the Institution. This was a huge relief, as all was not lost. I had a place to continue my education and swim.

Setting out for school in September of 2004, I had never been to Massachusetts, but it didn't matter. It was comforting to have somewhere to go after everything that I had been through. Swimming was firmly on the back burner, but I vowed to swim for the College. I had no intention of competing for Bermuda in International competition. Extremely damaged, I learned how to wear a mask. On the numerous occasions when the mask was challenged, anger would arise. Being a black swimmer in Massachusetts, I was subject to much ignorance and nonsense. Realizing quickly that 98% of the people around me had hardly traveled, it made no sense holding anything against them.

At Springfield, I met Lauren and I was quickly enamored by her. She was a stellar student, one of the women's swim team captains and an all-around hard worker. She always held herself accountable to study and train to the best of her ability. Every member on the team had great respect for her. She despised slacking off and would make sure you'd hear about it. Her wide range of taste in music would be how we came to initially relate. I had purchased a Apple iPod and we would share the headphones. She is now my wife.

A year into our courting, we would become pregnant and she would eventually give birth to our first child in the summer of 2006. A daughter we named Serena would bring much joy into our lives. Together we were opened up to the challenges of parenting and relationships but we always maintained strong communication. This allowed our compassion for one another to always prevail. We now have our second child, a son named Xavier, who was born in the fall of 2012. He brings great balance to us with his gentle spirit.

After a year into fatherhood, the 2008 Olympic Games were swiftly approaching. I was in contention to compete as the male representative for Bermuda by way of universality. This allows one male and one female to compete in the sport of swimming, to uphold the Olympic movement. Training on my own, with little knowledge and less resources was challenging. I hardly raced leading into the Games and I would suffer for that. I had a mediocre showing and it became a disappointing ending to what I built up as the pinnacle of my career. Nevertheless, I was able to enjoy many of the sites and sounds of Beijing. There was still fire within to seek the opportunity again. Racing lasted less than a minute but this experience would last a lifetime.

From 2009 through 2011, I sought to be a part of a team that had a collective mindset of competing at the highest level. After much searching, reaching out, trials and denials I found myself headed toward North Carolina to train with Swim MAC - a well-established club team that had a reputation for success with age group swimmers. There was a pro team affiliated with them called Team Elite. There were few pro teams around the world and I was given the chance to swim part-time. My proficiency was not high enough to train with them full time. The rest of my hours were spent with their top tier high school swimmers. Within a few months, I improved enough to earn a spot at the 2011 World Championships. It was there I made the 2012 Olympic qualification.

Now, with a well-established team, I was on my way to the London 2012 Olympic Games. Training and racing were going relatively well despite not having full time elite coaching. I was consistently competing within the realm of the top American Olympic candidates, which boded well for my confidence. Moving into the Games something felt incomplete. Even though

I was stronger and faster than I had ever been, there was still a void within, which I could not understand. The London environment was highly energetic, another dream come true, yet I could not beat the feeling of emptiness. Having completed the race in a personal best time and a new Bermuda National record, I failed to make the semi-finals. This left me feeling discordant and deeply frustrated. Four more years of my life had been dedicated to one goal, which I would not accomplish. The quadrennial is an unforgiving process. It is a daily grind that starts off at the pace of a snail and finishes like a high speed car chase. The volume starts low and tranquil then ends at the maximum decibels.

In January of 2015, my comprehension for the sport had finally reached a level of mastery. Each training session became a noble conquest. All my doubt and anguish were replaced with trust and fulfillment. Confidence was pulsating from my heart with an eager and ferocious desire to work. Feeling superhuman, it was as if fatigue no longer existed. My mind could push my body to its absolute brink.

The beginning of the end began on March 27, 2015, with a devastating knee injury. This was fifteen months prior to the 2016 Rio Olympic Games. I suffered a bilateral patellar tendon rupture, which required emergency surgery. Unable to walk for several months, it was imperative to elevate my mental strength. Through my tremendous support system, I was able to get back on my feet and address my training needs accordingly. This injury propelled me toward a new state of awareness. On the last days of the qualification period, I made the invitational standard for the Games but I had been superseded by a younger member of the Bermuda National Team. Devastated by the final result and out of time I hit a downward spiral and needed to seek counsel. Here would begin my path to enlightenment.

Part 1

Leaving The Shore

Awareness is a powerful acumen. By increasing awareness, we can better determine, 'what is'. When entering a new environment it creates a guiding light. Realize that newness is ever arising as we move through life. Firstly, compassion for yourself is imperative. It cultivates the seed of awareness for those with whom we interact. Enter a proactive state of being rather than a reactive one. This can be challenging, but with practice and patience it is achievable. Everyone moves through life differently, so relating to someone doesn't require you to have something tangible in common. The main thing we have in common is that we are all human. Shared interests have its appeal, but when it's used in the wrong way, it backfires on us. We have this uncanny ability to see what we want. Our habits keep us locked into a cycle that can be damaging at times. Plant the seed of awareness and tend to it accordingly.

Into The Night - Darkness Consumes Light

Between Worlds - Balance Meets Barriers

Unknown Formations - Mystifying Elements Manifest

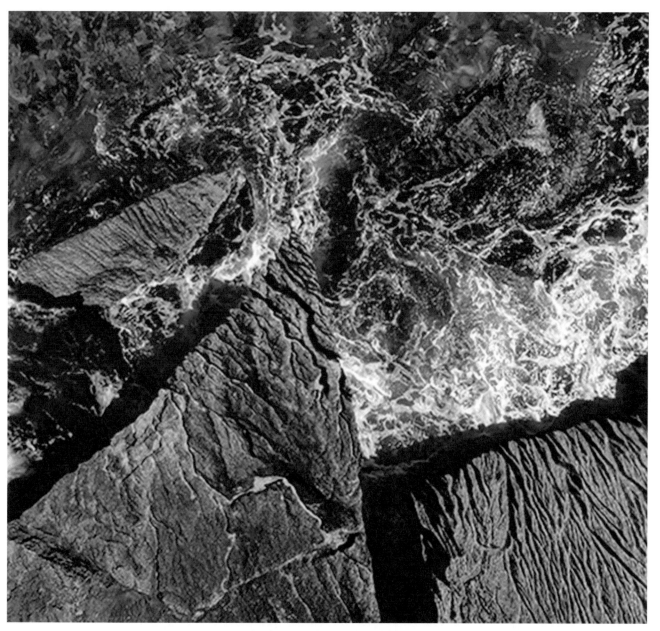

Jagged Edges - Sharpness Cuts Sensitivity

Muddy Waters - Clarity Is Lost

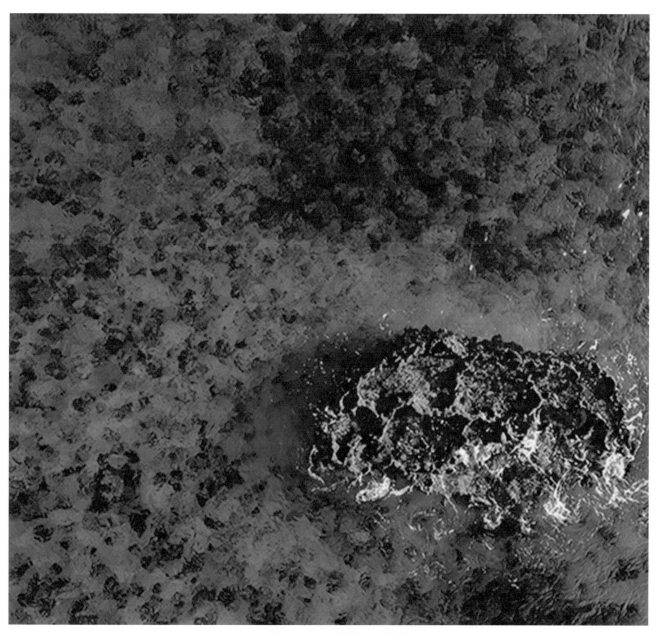

Worn - Time Takes A Toll

Glass Anchor - A Foundation Is Forming

Part 2

Explore

Utilizing your inner dimension is essential. The expansion within yourself is immense. Learn how elements of your life balance within the prodigious nature of your being. We cannot balance it all at once, so we must accept our place in the process. By allowing acceptance we have already made strides in the right direction. Notice yourself escaping your presence. If you are always escaping, then there is no joy. Open up to life and become available for opportunity. These opportunities show facets of ourselves that otherwise go undiscovered. When we can love ourselves where we are, awareness increases. We reap the energy needed to tackle what is. Dismantling our past takes away from our current realizations. Be patient with yourself as you explore and get to know all that you are.

On The Way - Allow More Learning

Undulation - Maneuver Through Environment

Converge - Connect The Dots

Aloneness - Energize Your Being

Resilience - New Found Strength

Emerge - Come Into View

Transition - Everything Touches Everything

Part 3

Discover

Many people are unaware of their life experience, which makes perspective limited. Since we cannot fathom all that we are, come to the realization that there are always parts of yourself unexplored. To realize that you are enough gives an infinite amount of space to move forward. Practice moving through the day with the least resistance. It unlocks an awareness to handle life as it's presented. Presence does not mean that you will be fully absent of struggle. It ultimately means, that you understand, you are more than your struggle. Come to discover an intense energy by channeling your thoughts into living presently. Validation from the outside world is not a sustainable source of energy. In the long run it will deplete, then defeat you. To be here now is an amazing feeling. One can be anywhere. One can be everywhere. One can be nowhere but one cannot be without self.

Hidden Tracks - Discover Roads Unknown

Together - Clarity Illuminates Support

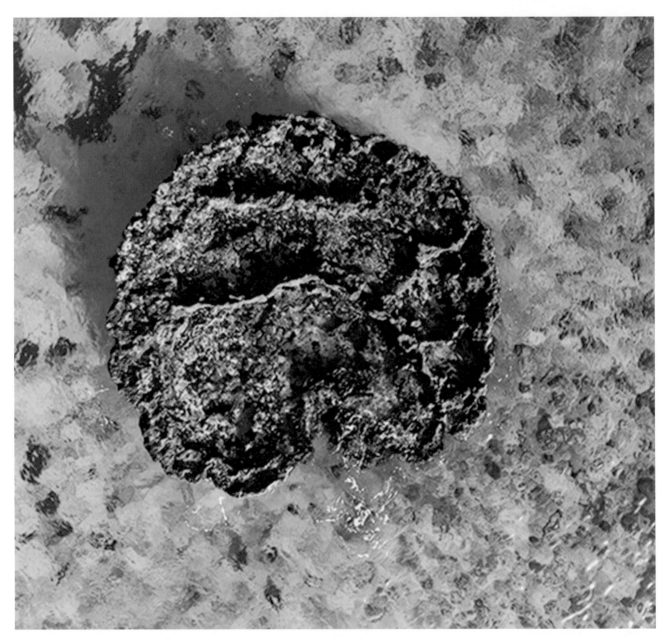

Balance - Center Is Found

Flow - River Runs Steadily

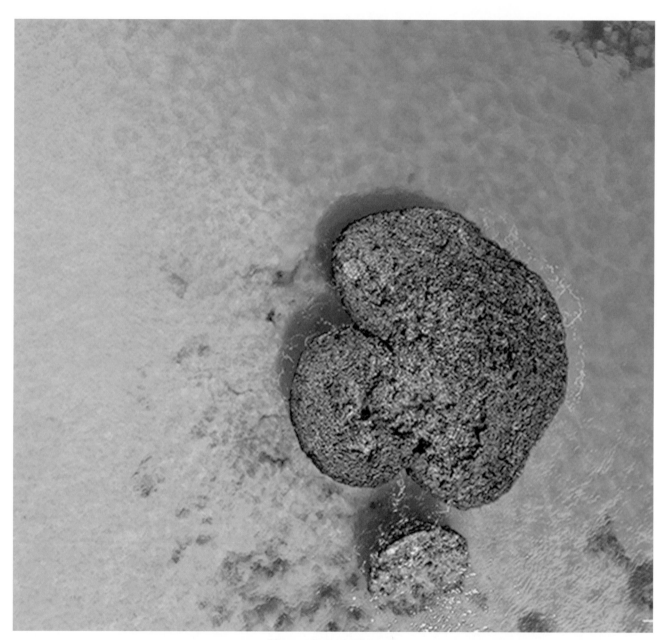

Heart - Love Is Exercise

Stairway to Heaven - Ascend The Path

Heaven - Presence Is Key

Part 4

Journey

A great difficulty manifests in a ones life when one becomes attached to something that doesn't exist. It leaves one only with what ifs, and what could've been. In society we acquire countless labels. Some that we give ourselves and others that are cast upon us. Once we are alone, none of those labels are pertinent. Many have reached the peaks of financial and material success yet still search for purpose. When we see clearly we know that no one is without struggle. The way people remember us is interesting. Parts of yourself left with them, are their own experience, perspective, and memory. Accept criticism as a mirror to reflect that person's view of themself. You don't have to immediately find meaning in everything as this can create a false outlook. Develop the courage to build patience and strength to take on your demons and defeat them. Change the definition of success from material gain, to understanding the ineffable nature of you.

Dream - Life Is The Goal

Sight and Vision

Sight showed him something was wrong.
Vision told him he needs to make a change.
Sight showed him what was on the surface.
Vision told him to dig deeper.
Sight showed him signs along the journey.
Vision told him to learn from the journey.
Sight showed him the destination.
Vision reminds him he is the destination.

Afterword

Journeying to Bermuda is a spiritual phenomenon. Your awareness spikes fifteen to twenty miles away as you begin to see the marvelous reef line. Progressing closer, you gaze at a view of the whole island. Therein lies an unanticipated coral land mass in the middle of the ocean. A blue sapphire radiating from the depths of darkness. The island's shape resembles a hook, which will catch you. The white roofs refract the radiance of the sun. Immediately you know you are somewhere special. The land is gorgeous between an endless ocean. The water so clear you can see directly to the bottom. This is a place where bright is brightest and where beauty is more beautiful - as we would say 'Bermudaful.' As you explore, you shall discover and learn a deeper part of your being. You will understand your calmness and your peace. You will witness your beauty and extravagance. Your heart and mind will open to the unknown spaces within. Allow the essence of the island to transcend your soul.

Noteable Competitions

2002 Commonwealth Games (Manchester, England)
2007 Fina World Championships (Melbourne, Australia)
2007 Pan American Games (Rio De Janeiro, Brazil)
2008 Olympic Games (Beijing, China)
2009 Fina World Championships (Rome, Italy)
2010 Caribbean and Central American Games (Mayaguez, Puerto Rico)
2010 Commonwealth Games (New Delhi, India)
2011 Fina World Championships (Shanghai, China)
2011 Pan American Games (Guadalajara, Mexico)
2012 Olympic Games (London, England)
2013 Fina World Championships (Barcelona, Spain)
2014 Commonwealth Games (Glasgow, Scotland)
2014 Caribbean and Central American Games (Vera Cruz, Mexico)
2014 Fina World Championships (Doha, Qatar)
2016 Caribbean Island Championships (Nassau, Bahamas)
 *last competition

Bermuda National Records (2019)
50m Freestyle LCM (22.47)
100m Freestyle LCM (50.26)
50m Butterfly LCM (24.77)
50m Backstroke LCM (28.14)
50m Freestyle SCM (21.81)
100m Freestyle SCM (48.56)
50m Backstroke SCM (26.56)
50m Butterfly SCM (24.26)

Springfield College Records (2019)
50y Freestyle SCY (20.26)
100y Freestyle SCY (45.08)
100y Backstroke SCY (51.28)

Printed in the United States
By Bookmasters